Fold & Fly

PAPER
AIRPLANES

TEXT by **MARK ZAGAESKI**

ILLUSTRATIONS & DESIGN by **ROB WALL**

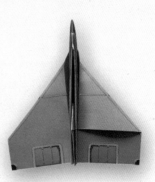

ROCKPOINT

ROCK POINT

First published in 2014 by Rock Point Publishing
an imprint of The Quarto Group
142 West 36th Street, 4th Floor
New York, NY 10018, USA
T (212) 779-4972 F (212) 779-6058
www.QuartoKnows.com

ROCK POINT and the distinctive Rock Point logo
are trademarks of Quarto Publishing Group USA

Rock Point titles are also available at discount for retail, wholesale, promotional, and bulk purchase. For details, contact the Special Sales Manager by email at specialsales@quarto.com or by mail at The Quarto Group, Attn: Special Sales Manager, 401 Second Avenue North, Suite 310, Minneapolis, MN 55401 USA.

TEXT Mark Zagaeski
ILLUSTRATION & DESIGN Rob Wall

GLIDER, EAGLE, DIAMOND & HAWK folds by Nick Robinson

Select photos are used with permission from:
da Vinci sketches © Luc Viatour / www.Lucnix.be,
kite © Wikimedia Commons/User:Tholly, propeller © iStock.com/MaRoPictures,
pg.6-7 diagrams: PD-old-100, pg.7 B-2 Bomber images: PD-USGov,
G. Cayley portrait, D. Bernoulli portrait by Johann Jakob Haid: Not-PD-US-URAA

This book is part of the FOLD & FLY PAPER AIRPLANES boxed set
and is not to be sold seperately.

ISBN: 978-1-63106-038-0

Printed in China

7 9 10 8

CONTENTS

PAPER PLANES for EVERY DAY

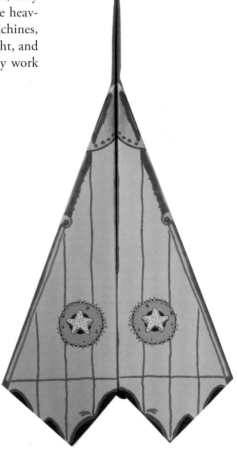

To fly! Nearly every one of us has wanted to leave the ground and soar through the skies, and throughout history birds, bats, insects, and falling leaves have inspired dreams of that experience in humans. Some of the first human-made flying devices were crafted from paper. Although these paper planes were too small to carry a person, they were large enough to carry the imagination into the heavens. Let's explore the history of these paper flying machines, some of the principles behind the magic of their flight, and a description of several paper designs and why they work as they do.

A BRIEF HISTORY
of the PAPER PLANE

Paper has been used as a material for constructing flying devices for thousands of years. Because it is both light and very strong for its weight, it is ideal for building devices that can be lifted by the force of moving air alone.

Paper was invented in China over two thousand years ago, and the Chinese have been using it for the earliest known flying application, kites, almost as long. The origin of the folded paper glider is uncertain, but given the refinement to paper construction that is origami, it is assumed that paper gliders were among the early models constructed by both Chinese and Japanese paper artists.

Chinese kite

Moving to the Western world, in the 1400s Leonardo da Vinci produced drawings of a flying device he called an ornithopter. Constructed from parchment (an early writing material) and wood, it was meant to carry a person. However, his device bore little resemblance to what we think of as a paper airplane, since it relies on a human flapping bird-like wings to keep the craft in the sky, rather than the graceful gliding of a folded-paper shape, gently falling to the earth.

da Vinci's ornithopter design

da Vinci's sketches

Jumping ahead to 1800, the English squire Sir George Cayley developed the concepts behind the modern airplane. He experimented with these concepts using gliders that were essentially kites, which he launched into the air to let fly freely. He constructed these gliders from linen (not quite paper) and wood, and from these experiments identified the four forces involved in flight: the opposing pair of lift and weight, thrust and drag. We will have more to say about these forces a bit later.

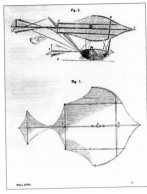

Sir George Cayley's "Governable Parachute"

Perhaps the first official record of a true paper airplane was a patent registered in 1867 by a pair of Englishmen, J. W. Butler and E. Edwards. Their patent described a folded paper glider that resembled the simple paper airplane nearly all of us made as children. American schoolchildren were folding these paper planes on the other side of the Atlantic by the early 1900s.

J.W. Butler and E. Edwards patented paper plane design, circa 1867. Envisioned with a form of propulsion, it's notably similar to the standard "dart" used today.

Paper models continued to be used by flight innovators, including the Wright brothers, who experimented with paper planes in a windtunnel while developing their infamous aircraft. In the 1930s, Jack Northrop (who cofounded the Lockheed Aircraft Company and later founded the Northrop Corporation) used paper models to investigate the principles of flight and help design the airplanes he was working on. His experimentation with tailless aircrafts called "flying wings" led to the design of the B-2 Spirit Stealth Bomber, which looks much more like a folded paper plane than it does a conventional aircraft.

B-2 Spirit Stealth Bomber

Due to the shortages of metal during World War II, toys made from paper became popular. Starting in 1944, General Mills published a set of paper models of the current World War II fighter airplanes, designed by Wallis Rigby. An English toy model maker, Rigby, introduced the "tab-in-slot" construction design for paper models. The model planes flew so well that they inspired a set of flight competitions in the United States.

In the late 1980s a Japanese aeronautics engineer, Dr. Yasuaki Ninomiya, designed a series of paper gliders he called White Wings. The original paper gliders feature layers of heavyweight paper cut out and glued together to make sturdy structures for both body and wings. Dr. Ninomiya drew on flight science and wind tunnel testing to develop the designs for these paper planes and so achieved remarkable flight performance for paper models. The modern versions of White Wings use pre-cut balsa wood bodies, and so are not strictly paper planes.

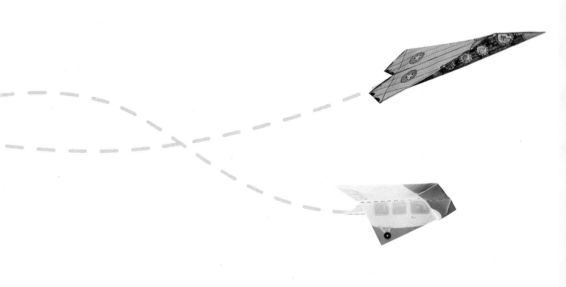

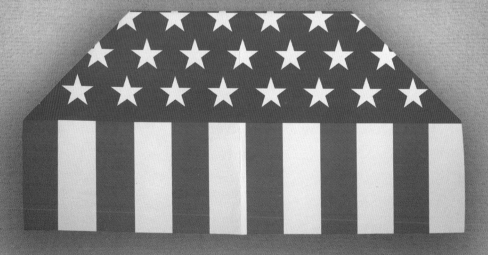

The PHYSICS of FLIGHT

Looking at a commercial airliner, it's hard to understand how such an incredibly heavy machine filled with people could really lift into the air and fly. To understand how this works, we must consider the two opposing pairs of forces, first described by George Cayley: the vertical forces of weight and lift, and the horizontal forces of thrust and drag.

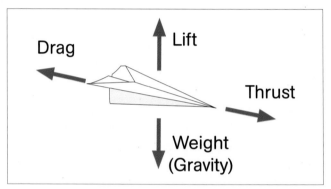

Fig. 1 - Four forces on a plane

In order for an object that is denser than air to lift off the ground, there must be a force on it greater that the object's weight. Not surprisingly, this force is called lift. For an airplane, that lift force is provided by creating a higher pressure under the plane (usually under the wing of the plane) than above it. This difference in pressure provides an upward push, which can balance the weight and either hold the plane in level flight or allow it to climb or descend if the upward push is adjusted. So how does an airplane create the differing pressures that produce lift? The details of this are still a matter of some debate among scientists, and lift can be explained in a number of ways. We will look at two simple ideas that explain most of the important features of how lift is generated.

George Cayley

The first explanation relies on a simple idea that was described by the Swiss mathematician and physicist Daniel Bernoulli. He discovered that the pressure in a fluid (like air) decreases as the fluid moves faster. You can demonstrate this easily by holding up two pieces of paper facing each other and blowing between them: the sheets will move together as the fast-moving air lowers the pressure between them.

Daniel Bernoulli

The classic airplane wing has a shape known as an airfoil with a rounded top surface and a flat bottom surface (see the drawing in Figure 2 - Airfoil). As the air streams over the wing, the air moves over the top faster than it moves under the bottom. Since the speed of the air is faster over the top than under the bottom, the pressure above is lower than the pressure below, and this pressure difference pushes the wing upward, producing the force of lift. The exact reason that the air moves faster over the top is what scientists still debate, but all agree that it is not just the simple idea that the air above the wing has farther to travel in the same time as the air along the bottom, since it has been shown that the air moves over the top even faster than that simple idea would predict.

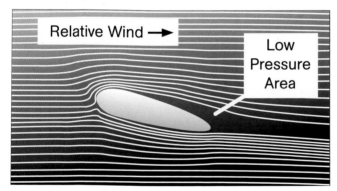

Relative Wind →

Low Pressure Area

Fig. 2 - Airfoil

"But," you say, "most paper airplanes have flat wings, so how do they produce lift?" The answer is that a paper plane falls as it moves through the air. This leads to two effects, both of which can contribute to keeping a paper plane aloft. One source of lift is very much the same as that described for a classic airplane wing. If a flat, thin wing moves horizontally through the air, then we can imagine that the air moving both over the wing and the air moving under the wing is virtually undisturbed by the presence of the wing. However if the path of the plane moves slightly downward as it moves through the air, then it is as if the air is hitting the wing from below, as in Figure 3.

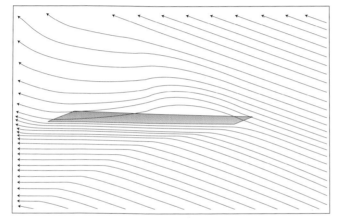

Fig. 3 - Flat wing in airstream

As air passes over the leading edge of the wing, the stream pulls away from the top surface of the wing a bit and therefore travels faster than the air under the bottom surface. The air passing under the wing is squeezed together and slows a bit, and, as with the curved airplane wing, this unequal speed leads to a higher pressure below the wing than above and that pressure difference provides lift. If the plane is angled up too sharply compared to the airstream, the air moving over the top of the wing can pull completely away from the surface of the wing, and this creates turbulence. Turbulence is the enemy of lift. Since it forms a region of slower-moving, swirling air above the wing, it destroys the pressure difference that created lift. When this happens, we say the plane is stalling.

The key to understanding the second effect explaining lift is Newton's third law: any force delivered to one object results in an equal and opposite force pushing back on the other object. As an example, imagine that you are standing on roller skates facing a wall. If you put your hands on the wall and try to push the wall away from you, you will find that the wall has actually pushed YOU just as hard as you have pushed it and you move backward. If you think carefully, you will realize that all forces have their equal and opposite partners acting on the other object in the pair.

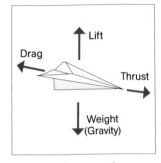

Fig. 1 - Four forces on a plane

Returning to Figure 3, if the air hits the wing from below, then the bottom of the wing pushes the air down as the wing passes through the air, and as a result the wing is pushed up. Think of riding in a car with your hand out the window: tilting the front edge of your hand upward will cause the wind to make your arm rise. If you tilt the front edge down, the wind pushes your arm downward. As long as a flat wing moves in such a way that air is striking it from below, the air is pushed down and the wing will in turn be pushed up against gravity.

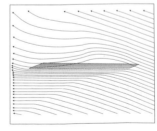

Fig. 3 - Flat wing in airstream

Now returning to Figure 1, let's consider the other pair of forces that Cayley identified to understand flight: thrust and drag. For a powered airplane, the thrust is provided by a propeller or a jet engine, and the drag force refers to the air resistance that acts in a direction opposite to the motion, which tends to slow the plane down. The faster a plane flies, the stronger the drag force and the more thrust is needed to maintain that speed.

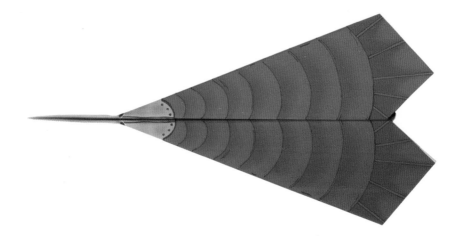

For a paper plane, the external thrust all occurs during the launch, and the momentum from that throw is carried forward as the plane travels through the air. The drag force constantly acts on the plane to slow it down during its entire flight. If all the thrust happens at the launch and the drag acts constantly on the flying plane, then why doesn't it just slow to a stop and fall out of the air? While the external thrust all occurs at the beginning of an airplane throw, there is a second, continuous form of thrust that keeps the plane moving forward so that the wings can develop the lift needed to keep it in the air.

Paradoxically, the gravity pulling the plane down is also its source of thrust, which pushes the plane forward through the air. To understand this, imagine a child on a playground slide. Gravity pulls the child straight down, but the slide pushes up against the child at an angle, so that the combined force pushes the child forward and down, causing her to speed up as she moves down the slide. So looking again at Figure 3, if the wing is tipped slightly forward, the air is pushed BACKWARD as well as downward, so that the upward push of air on the wings is tilted forward; just like the child on the slide, the plane is pushed forward as it falls. For a well-trimmed plane that is gliding to the ground, this small constant thrust from falling forward just balances the drag, and the plane doesn't speed up, it just moves forward at a constant speed, gently gliding to the ground. So you see, the lift and the thrust of a paper plane are inextricably linked to each other.

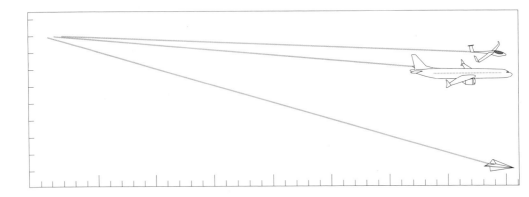

The ratio of how far a plane moves forward to how far it drops is called the glide ratio. Paper airplanes have glide ratios of about 5:1; in other words, the plane moves forward 5 feet for every foot it drops. By comparison, a full-sized, high-performance glider can have a glide ratio of 40:1 and a large commercial jet about 17:1.

Another way to understand the way weight and lift combine to cause a paper plane to fly forward is to introduce the ideas of center of gravity and center of pressure. Every object is pulled down to the Earth by gravity. If one end of a long object has more mass than the other (like the head end of a hammer), that part will be pulled down more strongly by gravity. If you were to put your finger under this object to balance it, you would need to put your finger closer to the heavier end. This balance point is directly below the center of gravity of the object. If you were to drill a hole through the object at the center of gravity, you could put a nail through that point and no matter which way you turned the object around the nail it would stay balanced. No matter how the object is turned, half of the mass would be on one side of the nail and the other half would be on the other side. So the center of mass of a paper airplane can be located by balancing the plane on your finger.

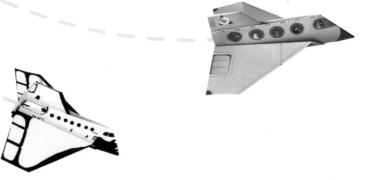

Now imagine holding a paper plane from underneath, with your thumb and forefinger. If you hold the plane over a fan that is blowing straight up, the plane will be pushed upward. If you hold it near the nose, the tail will pivot up in the breeze. If you hold it near the tail, the nose will pivot up. If you hold the spot along the body where the plane doesn't pivot (that is, where all the force from the wind is balanced) the place you are holding is at the center of pressure.

Most paper planes have their center of gravity just a bit forward of the center of pressure. If the plane is held flat and dropped, then as the plane starts to accelerate toward the ground the pressure increases, but the weight of the plane does not increase, and the unequal pushes tend to tip the nose of the plane forward slightly, pushing air out behind the plane, which pushes the plane forward. This is how a plane glides forward. The position of the center of gravity "in front of" the center of pressure defines the front of the plane. Try throwing a normal paper plane backward—none of the aerodynamics that let the plane glide works. It just flops over in the air.

FLIGHT CONTROL

For a paper plane to fly well, it needs to fly stably. In other words, it needs to maintain its orientation in the air as it moves forward, not flipping over or diving to the ground. There are three ways a plane can turn away from straight and level flight, and these are called roll, pitch, and yaw. Roll refers to the plane rolling over along its long axis, so the plane rolls when one wing lifts higher and the other drops. Pitch refers to the plane nose tipping down or nose up, and yaw refers to the plane turning its nose left or right while the body of the plane remains horizontal. A plane that is flying stably will return to level flight even if it is pushed off course slightly along any of these axes.

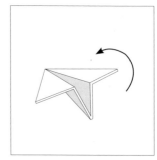

Roll

Each of these motions is affected by a particular characteristic of the plane or its wings. The process of making small adjustments to the folding of the plane to get it to fly stably is called trimming the plane. Trimming is an art more than a science, and the best way to learn to trim a plane is just to try it and see what works. The following ideas should help with your experimentation.

If a paper airplane rolls over into a spiral, then bending both wings upward slightly from horizontal (called the dihedral angle) will help to make the plane fly more stably. If the nose of the plane tips down so that the plane dives to the ground when it is thrown, then bending the back edge of both wings up slightly will give the plane more lift and correct that dive. If the nose of the plane tips up too much so that the plane goes straight up and stalls or flips over, then bending the back edges of the wings down slightly will correct that and level out the flight. It is rare for a paper plane to fly in such a way that it "yaws"—that the plane goes left or right without its body twisting—but if that were to happen, bending the rear vertical section of the plane to the opposite direction that the plane tends to go will straighten it out.

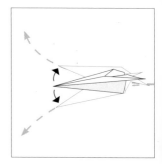

Pitch

Yaw

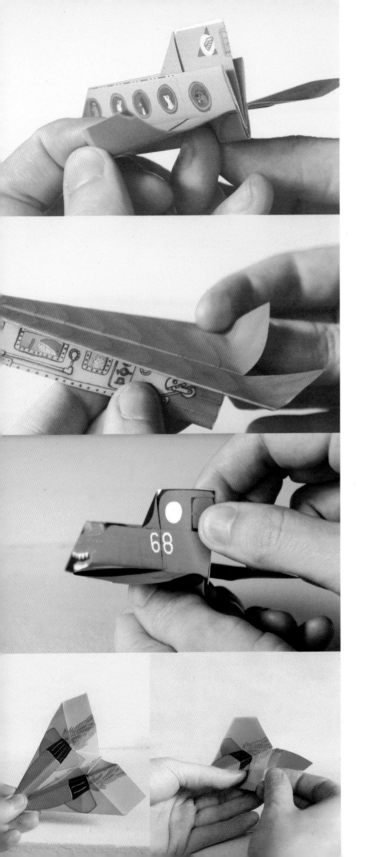

Bend the wings up slightly for more stable flight. If they're uneven, the plane will roll.

Bending the back edge of the wings upward will cause the plane to climb, or just keep the nose up. Bending them down will cause the nose to drop.

Adjust the rear vertical edge to compensate for yaw.

You'll find some of the more complex folds spring open, which can impair their flight. Feel free to tape the edges together for a more stable plane.

So we have discussed how a paper airplane can stay in the air and fly in a straight line. But how do we get a plane to do tricks? The same principles can be applied to make the plane roll, pitch, or yaw. For a plane to make a turn, the axis of the plane must tilt; in other words, it must roll slightly in the direction of the desired turn. Then the lift provided by the wings will be pointed slightly into the direction of that turn, with the result that the plane will move in a curve in that direction. The stronger the lift, the tighter the turn. For many paper planes, this can be accomplished simply by launching the plane tilted to the desired side. If you would like to make the turn tighter, simply trim it to give it more lift, by bending the back edges of the wings up a bit.

Fig. 4 - Paper plane tilted to turn

In order for a plane to climb and eventually make a loop, the nose of the plane must pitch upward as it flies. If the nose continually pitches upward, the plane will climb and eventually turn upside-down and continue to fly along that circle until it is flying level again. Some paper planes are designed to loop; these planes tend to have large wings for their size and a center of gravity that is closer to the center of pressure. If you want to trim a plane so that it will loop, you can cause it to fly nose-up by increasing the lift. You do this just as you do to correct a dive—by bending the rear of each wing slightly upward, but bend the edges more, so that it is overcorrected, and then it will loop. Usually, you will have to throw a plane a bit harder than normal to cause it to loop, so that the speed of the plane creates enough lift to pull it up and over.

Paper airplanes have fueled the human desire to explore flight for centuries and this brief overview has given you a taste of their history and the science behind their aeronautic magic.

The following pages will teach you how to fold some planes of your own, so you can take to the skies!

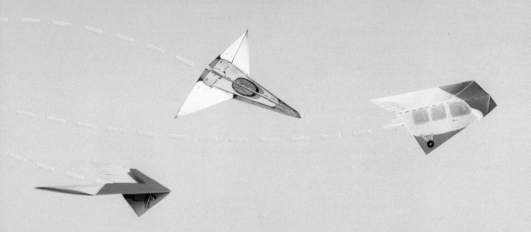

FOLD INSTRUCTIONS

GUIDE TO FOLDS:

The following pages have instructions for 12 different plane folds. Understanding the symbols here will make folding a breeze.

VALLEY FOLD: fold forward

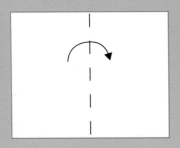 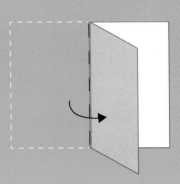

MOUNTAIN FOLD: fold backward

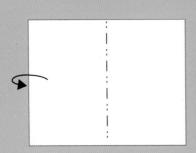 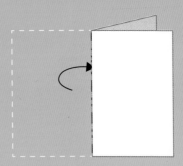

CREASE: from a previous fold

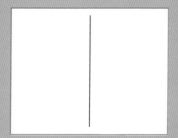

FOLD & UNFOLD: fold and then unfold to create a crease

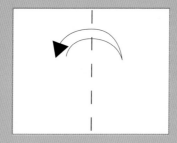

INVERT: create creases and push corner or edge in along folds

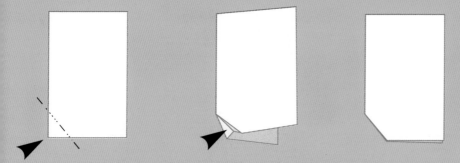

*Only one fold line is shown, but for best results,
crease both forward and backward.

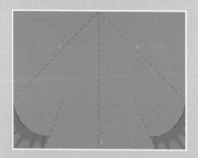 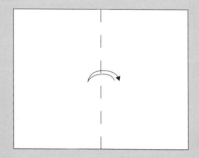

MATCHING PATTERNS:

An image of the corresponding patterns appears at the beginning of each fold instruction. Align the paper as shown in the first instruction to match the final fold.

RED FOLDS & BLUE CREASES:

Full folds are labeled with RED numbers.
Creases are labeled with BLUE numbers.

SIMULTANEOUS FOLDS:
Some steps will cover 2 or more folds. Each of which will be labeled with the step's number on the sheet.

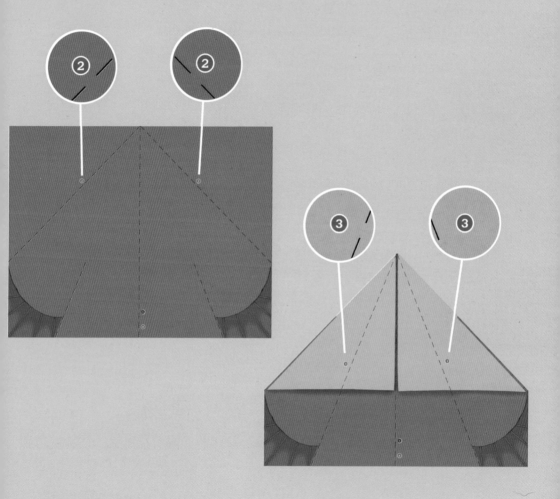

UPRIGHT NUMBERS:
The numbers should appear upright when the paper is aligned with the directions.

Dart Jet

1

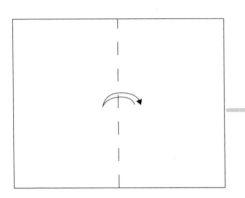

Make crease by folding in half.

2

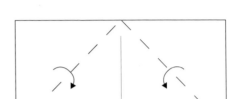

Fold top corners down
to the center crease.

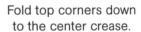

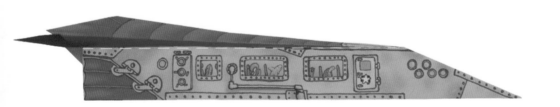

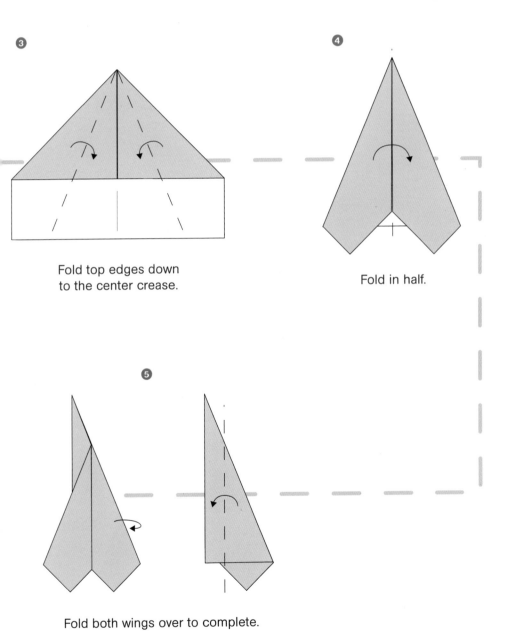

❸ Fold top edges down to the center crease.

❹ Fold in half.

❺ Fold both wings over to complete.

Glider

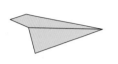

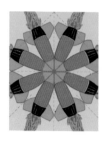

❶

Make crease by
folding in half.

❷

Fold top corners down
to the center crease.

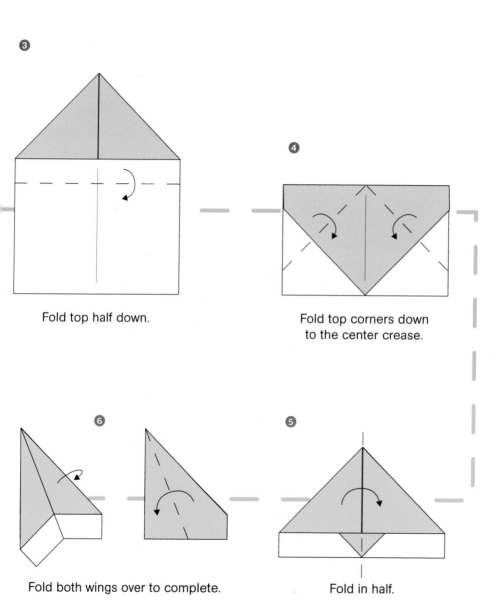

3

Fold top half down.

4

Fold top corners down
to the center crease.

6

Fold both wings over to complete.

5

Fold in half.

Eagle

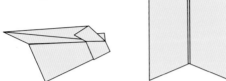

1

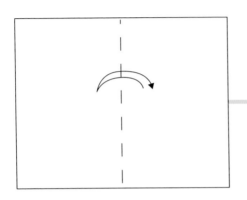

Make crease by
folding in half.

2

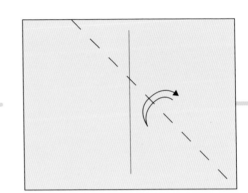

Make crease by folding the
right edge down to the
bottom edge.

8

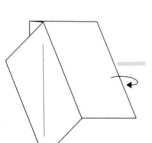

Fold both wings over to complete.

7

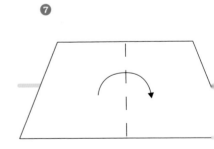

Turn over and fold in half.

3

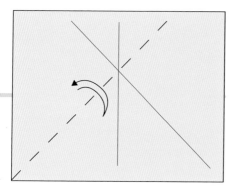

Make crease by folding the
left edge down to the
bottom edge.

4

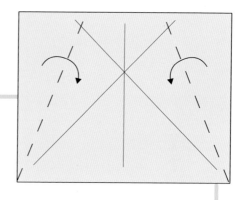

Fold left and right sides
over to align with
diagonal creases.

6

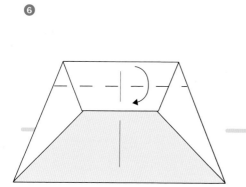

Fold top down again.

5

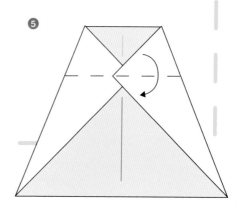

Fold top down as shown.

Albatross

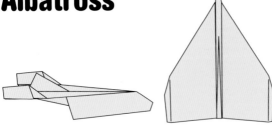

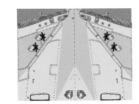

1

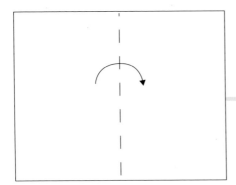

Fold in half.

2

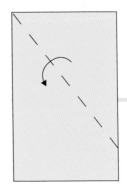

Fold top right corner down as shown, extending slightly beyond the left edge.

7

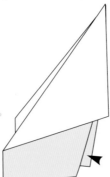

Invert corner along crease.

6

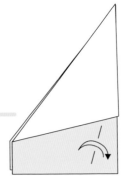

Create a crease on the center layer as shown.

continued on page 38...

❸

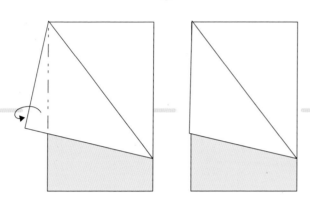

Fold overhanging flap under,
so that the left edge is straight.

❺

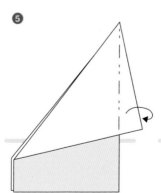

❹

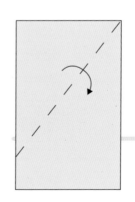

Fold overhanging flap
under so that the right
edge is straight.

Turn over and repeat
on opposite side.

...continued from page 36

8

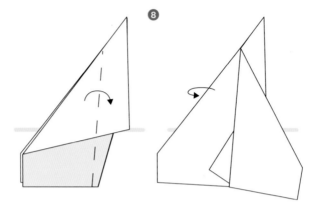

Fold both wings over.

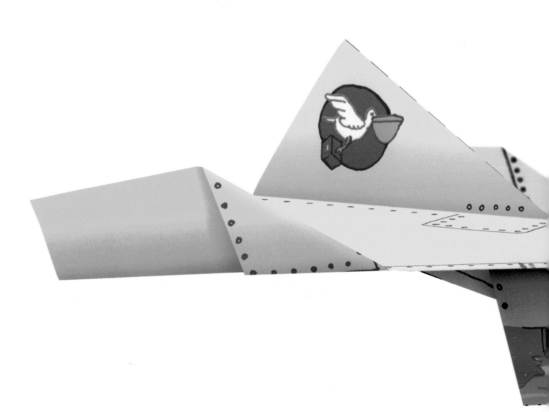

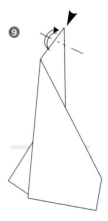

Create crease
and inverse tip.

Fold up the ends
of the wings to
complete.

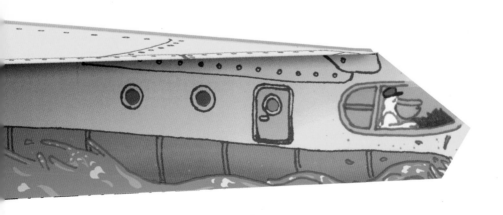

Diamond

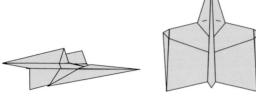

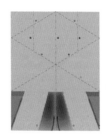

Fold in half.

❷

Create creases at 1/4 the
width of the page by folding
the sides to the center crease.

❻

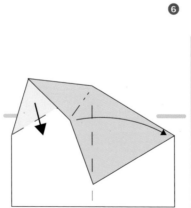

Fold the left point of the flap
over to the right side as shown.

continued on page 42...

❸

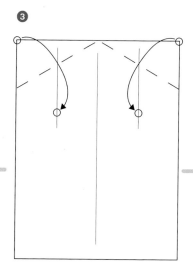

Fold top corners down to
the 1/4 width creases.

❺

❹

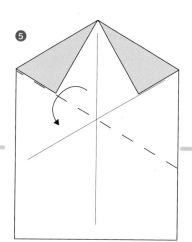

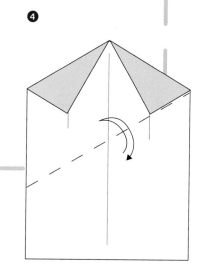

Fold the top right
portion down along the
edge of the right flap

Create a crease by folding the
top left portion down along the
edge of the right flap.

...continued from page 40

❼

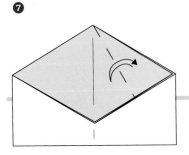

Create a crease by folding
the top of the right flap
down to the center crease.

❽

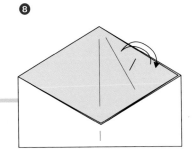

Create another crease by
folding the right point of the
flap up to the top point.

⑪

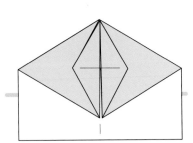

Use the creases you've
created to fold the bottom
point of the top flap upward
and flatten as shown.

continued on page 44...

9

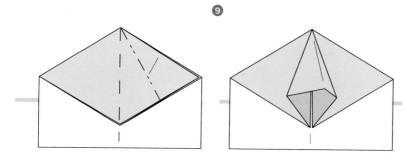

Use the creases you've created to
flatten the top flap as shown.

10

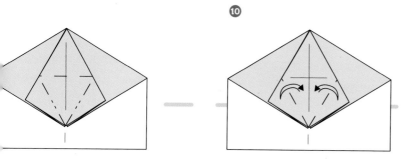

Create creases by bringing
the side points of the top
flap to the center crease.

...continued from page 42

12

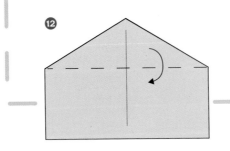

Turn over and fold top
downward as shown.

13

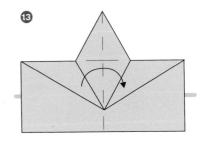

Fold in half.

15

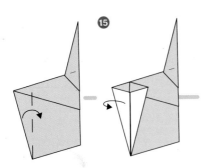

Complete by folding the
tips of the wings over.

14

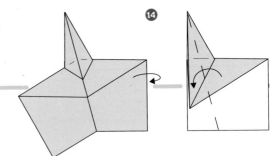

Fold the wings over as shown.

Hawk

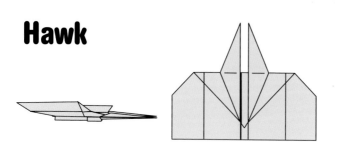

①

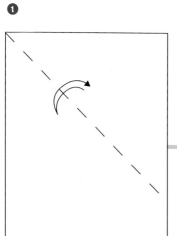

Create a crease by folding
the top edge down diagonally
to align with the left edge.

②

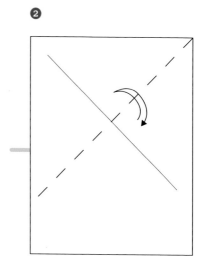

Create a crease by folding
the top edge down diagonally
to align with the right edge.

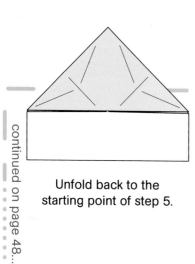

Unfold back to the
starting point of step 5.

⑤

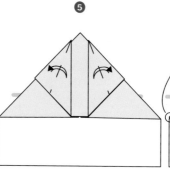

Create creases by
folding the new top
flaps in half as shown.

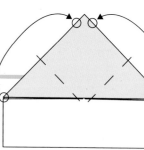

Fold the left and right poin
up as shown. Note that yc
are not folding all the way
the center high point.

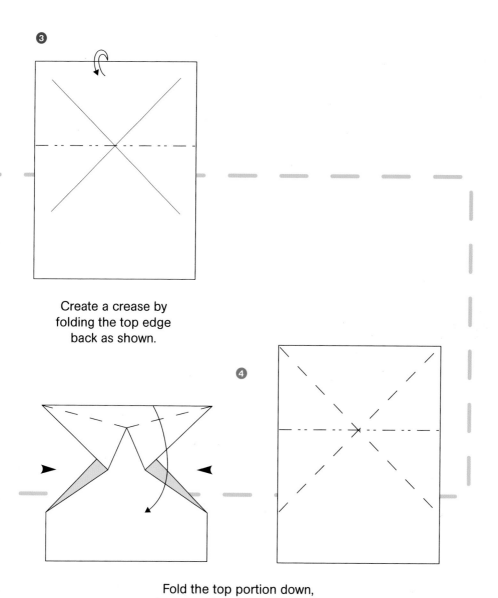

3

Create a crease by folding the top edge back as shown.

4

Fold the top portion down, inverting the sides as shown.

...continued from page 46

❻

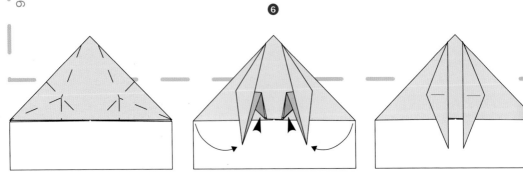

Use creases from step 5 to fold the left
and right points downward as shown.

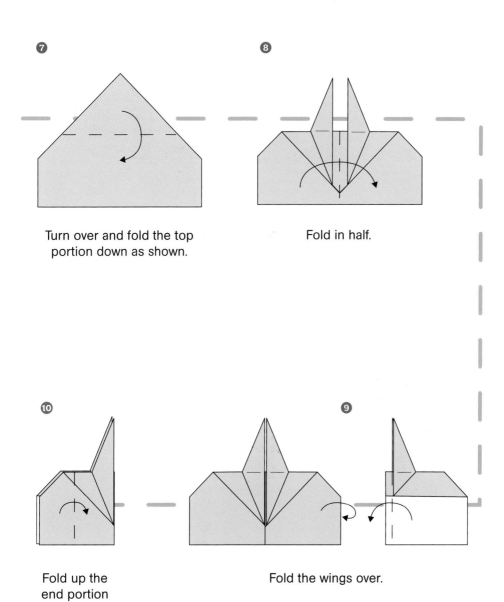

7 Turn over and fold the top portion down as shown.

8 Fold in half.

10 Fold up the end portion of the wings.

9 Fold the wings over.

Shuttle

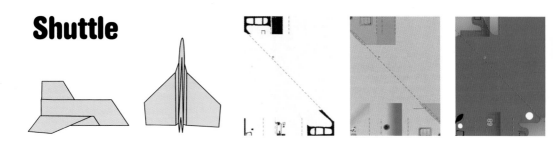

1

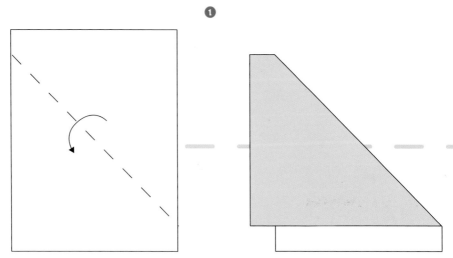

Fold diagonally, so equal lengths of paper
extend off the bottom and left sides.

5

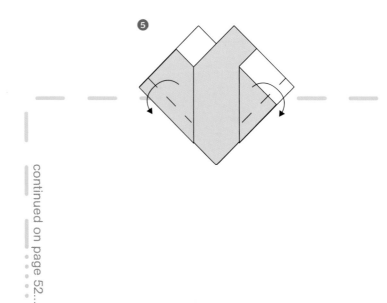

continued on page 52...

❷

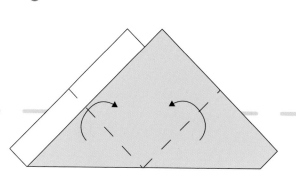

Rotate as shown and fold
the left and right points up
to the top.

❹

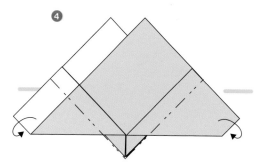

Fold overhanging flaps
under as shown.

❸

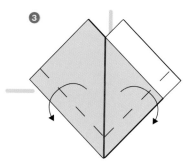

Fold the top portion of
the front flaps back down
as shown.

...continued from page 50

⑥

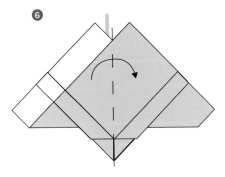

Turn back over and
fold in half.

⑦

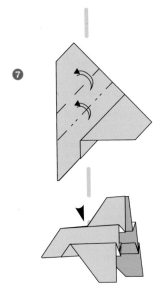

Create creases and invert
along folds as shown.

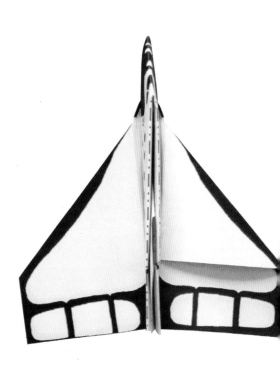

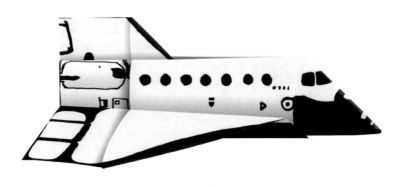

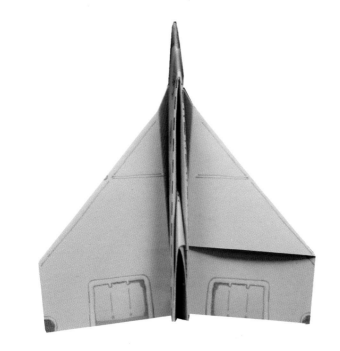

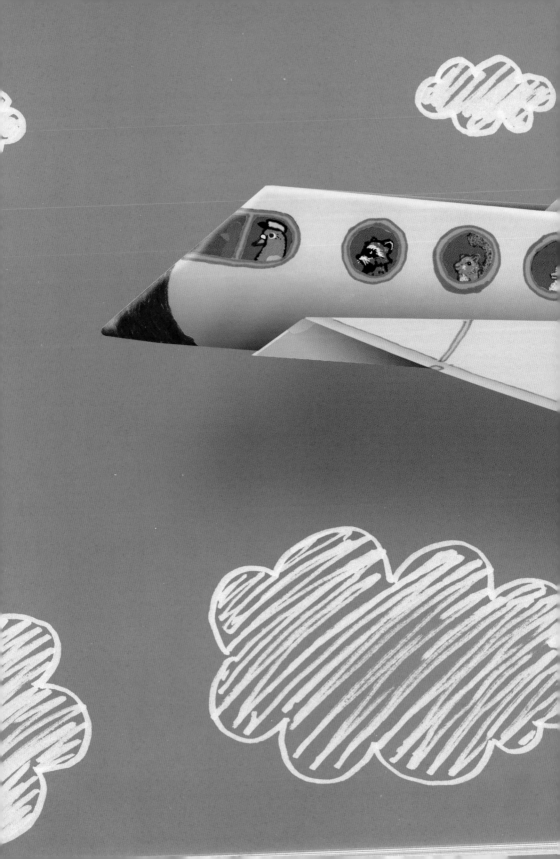

The Wing

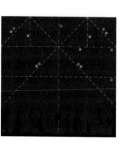

❶

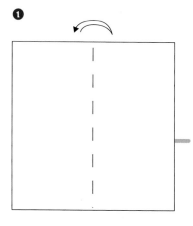

Create crease by folding the
sheet in half.

❹

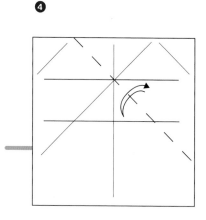

Repeat step 3 on the right
side to create another crease.

❸

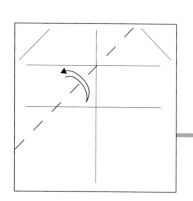

Create a crease by folding
diagonally as shown, with the
fold ending at the corner
crease created in step 2.

continued on page 58...

❷

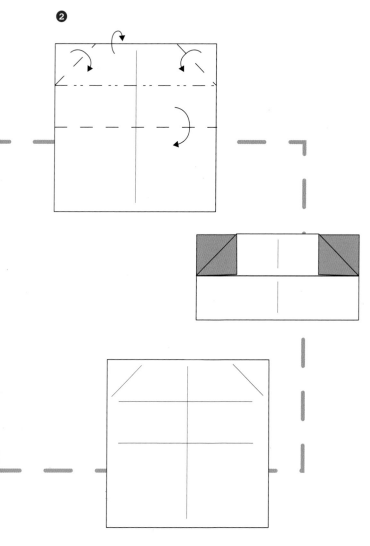

Create creases by making the
four folds shown above, then
flatten the paper out again.

...continued from page 56

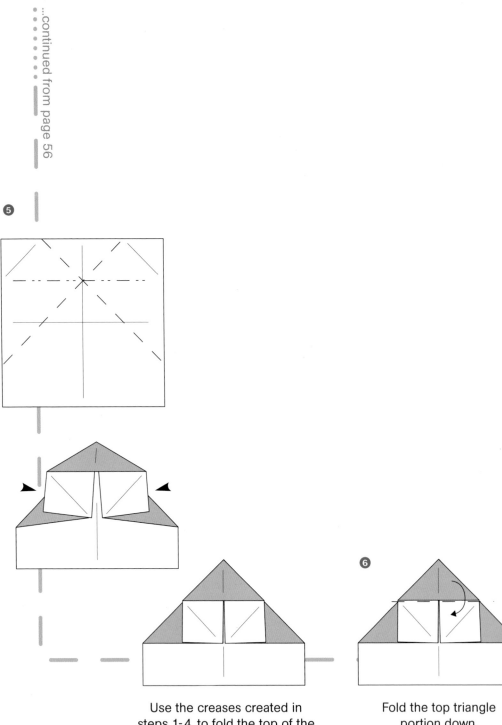

5

Use the creases created in steps 1-4 to fold the top of the sheet down, inverting the sides.

6

Fold the top triangle portion down.

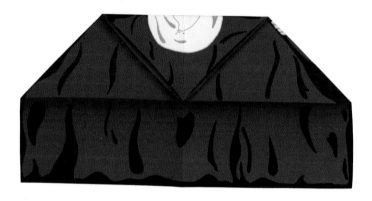

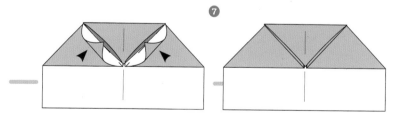

Fold the two loose triangle flaps up into the slits
on the side of the top flap, locking it into place.

Hang Glider

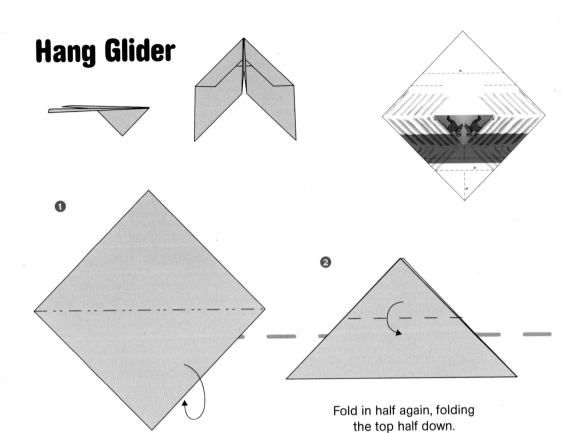

①

②

Fold in half again, folding
the top half down.

Start with the paper as
shown, and fold the bottom
half back.
(Note: the Guided Fold line for step 1
appears on the opposite side)

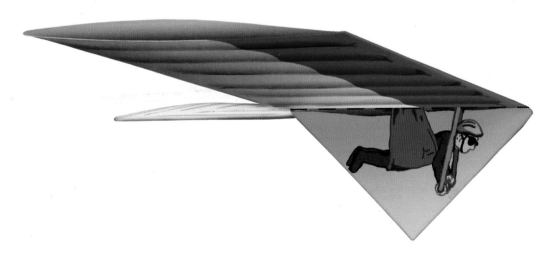

③

Fold the top edge
down as shown.

④

Fold in half.

⑤

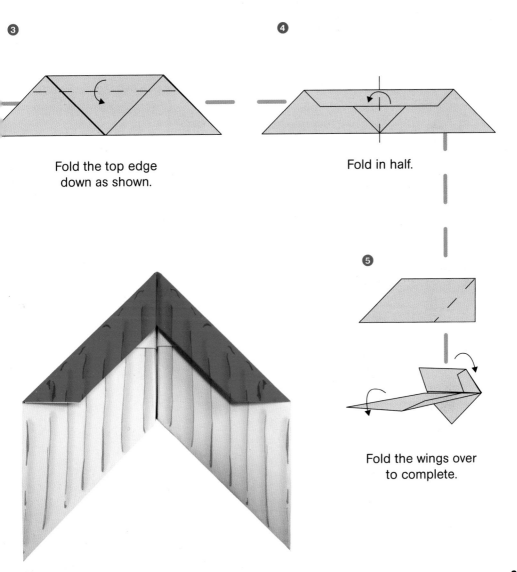

Fold the wings over
to complete.

Flying Box

❶

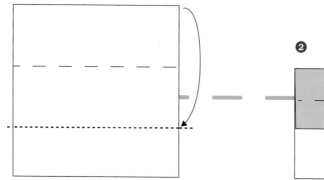
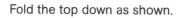

Fold the top down as shown.

❷

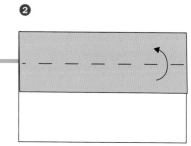

Fold the bottom half of the top flap upward.

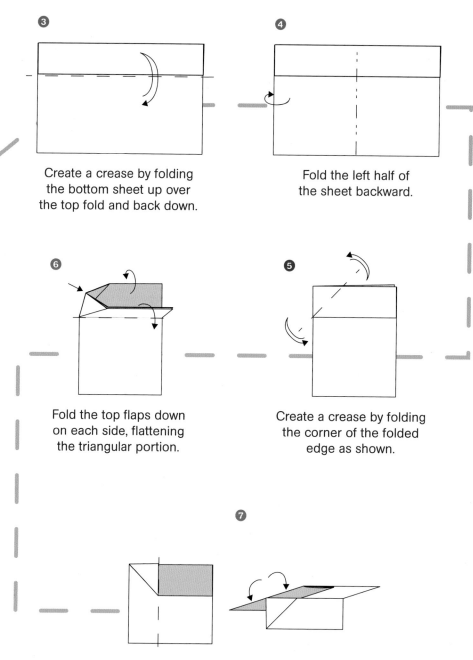

3

Create a crease by folding
the bottom sheet up over
the top fold and back down.

4

Fold the left half of
the sheet backward.

6

Fold the top flaps down
on each side, flattening
the triangular portion.

5

Create a crease by folding
the corner of the folded
edge as shown.

7

Fold the wings over to complete.

Stinger

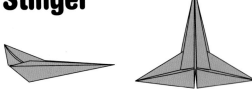

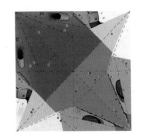

1

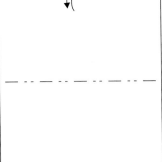

Create crease by folding top half back.

2

Create crease by folding the top right corner down to the lower left.

3

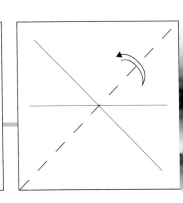

Create another crease by folding the top right corner down to the lower left.

7

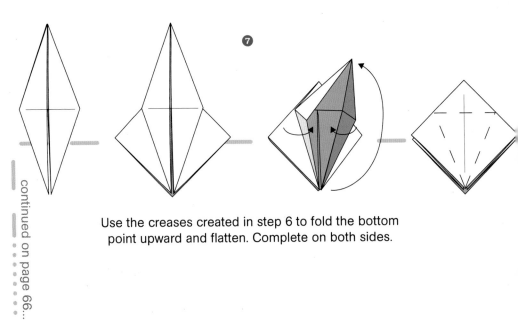

Use the creases created in step 6 to fold the bottom point upward and flatten. Complete on both sides.

continued on page 66...

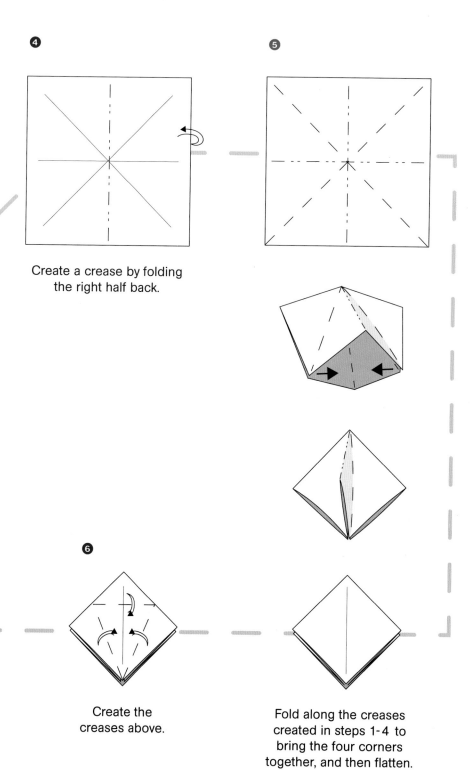

④

Create a crease by folding
the right half back.

⑤

⑥

Create the
creases above.

Fold along the creases
created in steps 1-4 to
bring the four corners
together, and then flatten.

8

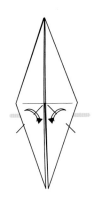
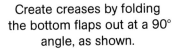

9

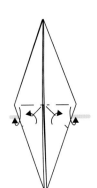
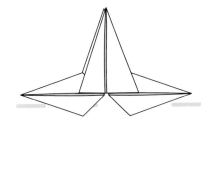

Create creases by folding the bottom flaps out at a 90° angle, as shown.

Using the existing creases, fold the bottom flaps up at a 90° angle, inverting one half, so it tucks inside the top fold.

11

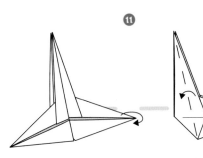

10

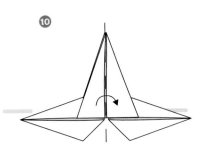

Fold out wings to complete.

Fold in half.

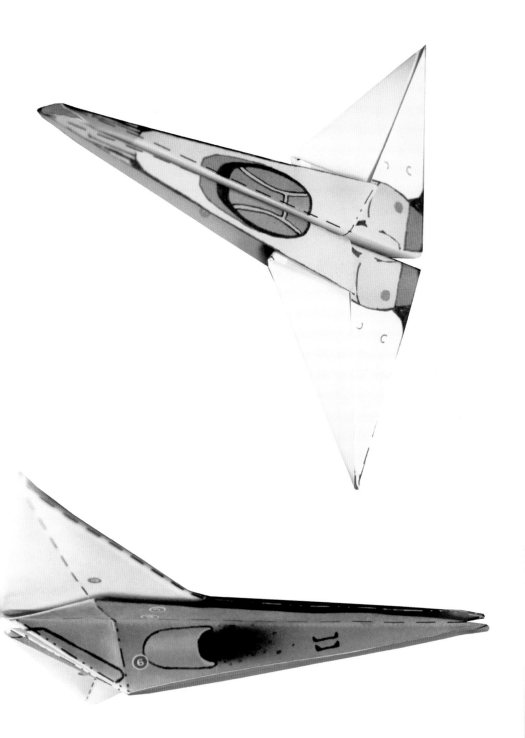

Sonic

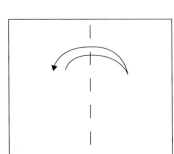

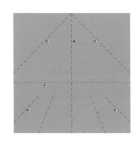

❶

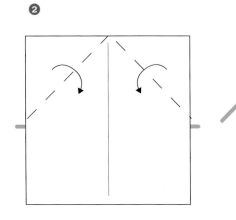

Fold sheet in half
to create crease.

❷

Fold the top corners down
to the center crease.

❽

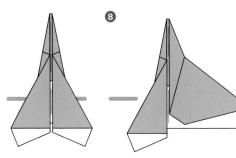

Repeat steps 6-7 on the right half.

❼

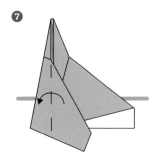

Fold the flap back to the
left at the center crease
line to create the wing.

continued on page 70...

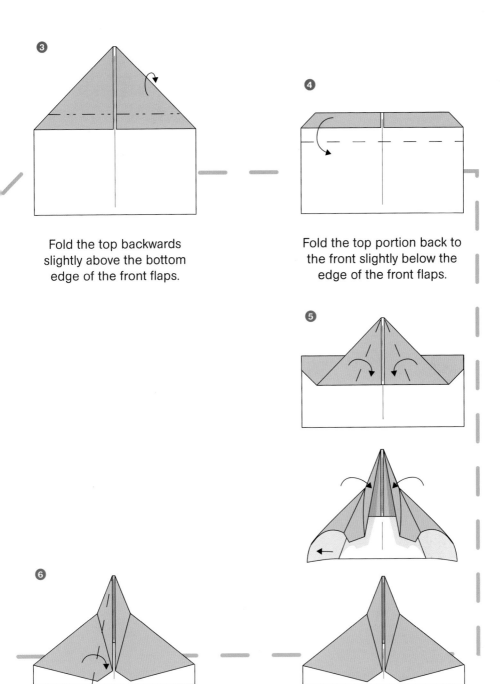

③ Fold the top backwards slightly above the bottom edge of the front flaps.

④ Fold the top portion back to the front slightly below the edge of the front flaps.

⑤

⑥ Fold the left portion over, aligning the edge of the narrow top section to the center crease.

Fold the top triangular folds in half as shown, while keeping the lower corners in place.

...continued from page 68

⑨

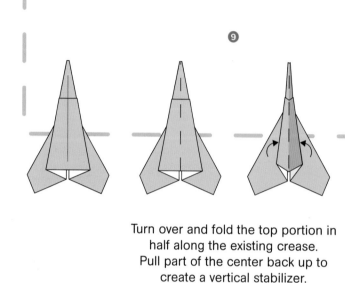

Turn over and fold the top portion in
half along the existing crease.
Pull part of the center back up to
create a vertical stabilizer.

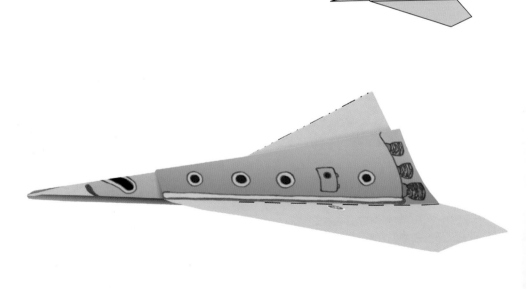